THE Divali Story

Text by Anita Ganeri 2003
Illustrations by Carole Gray
© copyright in this edition Tulip Books 2018

Printed in Malta by Melita Press

Acknowledgements:
For permission to reproduce copyright material, the author and publishers gratefully acknowledge the following:
page 20 Circa Photo Library/ John Smith
page 21 Circa Photo Library/ William Holtby

ISBN 978-1-78388-058-4

THE Divali Story

Anita Ganeri

Illustrated by
Carole Gray

Contents

Long ago, King Dasharatha ruled the kingdom
of Kosala in India. He was a good king, who
ruled wisely. Prince Rama was the eldest of his
four sons and he was the apple of his father's eye.
Rama married a beautiful princess, called Sita.
Filled with pride, King Dasharatha made Rama
heir to the throne. But Rama's stepmother had
other plans and went to see the king.

"Long ago, my Lord, I saved your life," she said, "and in return, you gave me two favours to ask of you whenever I liked. Now it is time to keep your promises. My first request is that you make my son, Bharata, king. My second is that you banish Rama to the forest for fourteen years."

The king was heartbroken but he kept his word, and Rama obeyed his wishes. He set off to the forest with Sita and his brother, Lakshman.

Many years passed. Rama, Sita and Lakshman lived happily in the forest and collected wild fruit and vegetables to eat. One day, Rama and Lakshman were out trying to catch a golden deer, which Sita had spotted among the trees. It was the most beautiful creature she had ever seen, and she wanted to keep it as a pet.

While Rama and Lakshman were gone, an old man came to the cottage door. He was dressed in the robes of a wandering holy man.

"Is anyone there?" the old man called, "to welcome a poor stranger?"

Sita opened the door and welcomed the holy man. She offered him a place to rest, and gave him something to eat and drink.

But the old man was no ordinary stranger. He was the terrifying ten-headed Ravana, the demon king of Lanka, in disguise. He had sent the golden deer to trick Rama and Lakshman, and keep them out of his wicked way. Ravana bundled Sita into his chariot and sped through the skies back to Lanka. Ravana had been told that if he married Sita, he would rule the world.

When Rama and Lakshman returned, they were filled with dismay. In despair, Rama called on the monkey army to help him find his wife. The monkeys searched high and low but they could not find Sita anywhere, until they met the vulture, Sampathi, at the southern tip of India.

"I can tell you where Sita is," the vulture croaked. "Ravana has carried her off to Lanka."

Lanka was an island, far out in the ocean. From their ranks, the monkeys chose the general, Hanuman, for the task of crossing the sea. Now Hanuman was no ordinary monkey, but the son of the god of the wind. He took a long jump and, in a single bound, leapt over to Lanka.

On he flew until he reached Ravana's palace. Then, as quiet as a mouse, he crept inside and found Sita in the palace garden, watched over by demon guards. Sita was overjoyed to see him and gave him her ring to take back to Rama.

"Please come back and rescue me soon," she whispered to Hanuman. "If I don't agree to marry Ravana, he has vowed to eat me up."

"Don't worry, my lady," promised Hanuman. "We will soon come back for you."

Then, bidding her farewell, he sped back over the sea to Rama and told him all that he had seen and heard.

When Rama and Lakshman heard Hanuman's news, they gathered a huge army of monkeys and bears, led by Hanuman and Jambhavan, king of the bears. Then they built a great stone bridge over the sea and marched to Lanka.

Meanwhile, in Lanka, Ravana's spies had told him that Rama was coming. He summoned all his best soldiers and sent them into battle.

"Don't come back until you've killed them all!" Ravana screamed after them.

All day and all night, the battle raged. Soon the air was thick with the soldiers' cries, and with arrows and spears flung from both sides.

By morning, the ground was red with blood. Hanuman wept as he looked over the battlefield and saw so many friends lying injured or dead. But worse was yet to come.

Suddenly, Hanuman spotted the bodies of Rama and Lakshman lying among the wounded. They had been struck by arrows fired by Indrajit, Ravana's eldest son. Fast as the wind, he flew over the forests, rivers and plains to the lofty Himalayas, to find the mountain where magical herbs grew. These herbs had special healing powers and could bring the dead back to life.

But Hanuman could not find the right herbs to pick so he lifted up the whole mountain instead and flew back to Lanka. Soon the sweet smell of the herbs wafted over the battlefield. Before long, not only were Rama and his brother brought back to health, but so were all the other soldiers who had fallen in battle.

Now, at last, it was time for Rama to face Ravana alone. Ravana put on his finest gold armour and a helmet on each of his ten heads. Then, with a blood-curdling battle cry, he raced off in his chariot towards Rama. But Rama was ready for him. Calmly, he fitted a golden arrow to his bow, took careful aim and fired. The arrow, a gift from the gods, struck Ravana straight in the heart. With a frightful shriek, the demon king toppled out of his chariot, dead.

Among the cheers and rejoicing, Sita came out of the palace to be reunited with Rama, her beloved husband. Then, together with Lakshman and the faithful Hanuman, they rode back home on a great swan, to be crowned king and queen.

Divali Celebrations

In October or November, Hindus celebrate the festival of Divali. This is a happy time when people remember the story of Rama and Sita and light divas, or oil lamps, to welcome the couple home. In India, Divali celebrations last for five days. In Britain, they take place over a weekend. During this time, people visit the mandir (temple), eat special food, and exchange cards and gifts. There are also spectacular firework displays.

The Ramayana

The story of Rama and Sita comes from a very long poem, called the Ramayana. It has 24,000 verses and is one of the Hindus' most sacred texts. The Ramayana is thought to have been composed some 5,000 years ago, although it was not written down until much later. It is still very popular today. In India, children can read the story in comic books, see

it acted out in plays, and watch it on television.

A Divali Recipe

At Divali and other Hindu festivals, people exchange gifts of sweets. They buy these from sweet shops or make them at home. You can find out here how to make your own coconut barfi (sweet) for Divali.

ASK AN ADULT TO HELP YOU

Ingredients:

1/4 litre milk
500 g granulated sugar
1 tablespoon butter
500 g dried milk powder
1/2 cup desiccated coconut
1/4 cup chopped nuts
(almonds and pistachios)

What to do:

1. Gently heat the milk in a saucepan. Add the sugar and stir until the mixture comes to the boil.
2. Add the butter, stirring all the time.
3. When the butter has melted, add the coconut and nuts.
4. Remove the mixture from the heat. Stir in the milk powder.
5. Lightly grease a baking tray. Pour the mixture in and spread it out evenly.
6. Leave the mixture for several hours until it is cool.

Then cut it into diamonds or squares and share it with your friends.

Happy Divali!

Making a Hanuman Mask

Join in the fun of Divali and try making this mask of
Hanuman, the general of the monkey army and
the son of the god of the wind.

You will need:

a sheet of thick brown cardboard
gold or yellow cardboard
coloured paper and crayons
a black marker pen
safe scissors
PVA glue
a long stick
strong sticky tape

What to do:

1. Cut out the
mask's shape from
the brown card,
using the picture
to help you.
Remember to
make it big enough
to cover your face.

2. Cut out Hanuman's face from the coloured paper and stick it onto the
head. Draw in the nose and the mouth.

3. Draw in the eyes and make small holes in the centre of them.

4. Cut out a crown from the yellow cardboard and a necklace and other
decorations from the coloured paper and stick them onto the mask.

5. Tape the stick onto the mask with strong sticky tape.
Now your mask is ready.